A Full Cup OF NosEEy Me

He Pours Down,

We Grow Up

Nita Hampton

Published and Distributed By
S. Hampton Foundation Publishing
Los Angeles, California
Email: smhampton1976@gmail.com

Packaging/Consulting
Professional Publishing House
1425 W. Manchester Ave. Ste B
Los Angeles, California 90047
323-750-3592
Email: professionalpublishinghouse@yahoo.com
www.Professionalpublishinghouse.com

Cover design and artwork by Shanita Hampton
First printing July 2021
978-1-7368493-2-3
10987654321

Special Thanks...

To a great son, Christopher.

Son, you have inspired me to look beyond the skin when you said, "Mom, why don't you look a little deeper?" I took your words, along with your happy energy off with me. Now this life journey means so much more to me.

Son, you are the reason I now believe in our family tree. I love all my family.

As I looked within myself, a rosebud was shown to me. The bud pinned up with emotions, alone with nothing to offer. Only to realize in due time the bud of the brain would blossom, refreshing the entire globe.

Dedications...

I dedicate this book to my family,. Margie (mother), Laqueta (sister), Maurice (brother), Kendra (sister), Daylan (brother), Marcella (sister), Starrla (sister), Tanesha (sister), with so many more family members to name. Thank you all.

Acknowledgments...

I want to thank the one and only Coach Ron, who always wanted the best for us.

Thanks to Brother Bryant for Pasadena Youth Christian Center.

Positivity over negativity is God's good energy.

Introduction...

A Full Cup of NosEEy Me is based on a true story. All my life I had my hand up asking questions. The need to know why, wouldn't let me sleep. Nosey people don't sit around, their wheels keep spinning round. The entire world happens to be my playground. Plenty rings of fire, but my heart had only one desire...Truth.

HE POURS DOWN, WE GROW UP

I was living here on earth, but feeling dead to the world. Now, how could that be, you wonder? It's like this, without me acknowledging or understanding my higher power, I couldn't find the joy I once had as a child. I noticed my joy leaving when I attended my grandfather's funeral. Realizing all my wild and fun days would be over, because I would no longer be able to hang out with my grandpops. On the day of his funeral, he didn't just die. My joyful spirit died right along beside him.

There's mental death, spiritual death, and physical death. Physical death is brought to us, and is understood by having a funeral. We hear about funerals all the time. Either someone in the world has died, or someone close to us. It's a sad thing. Some friend or family member has to get up and speak about how the person in the casket lived their life, and how much that person meant to them. While expressing their words, there's pain and hurt all in the air touching mostly everyone in the room, even some that couldn't make it, or were too weak to attend.

Death affects a lot of people on many different levels. A parent losing her child, or a child losing her parent, I believe, is the most extreme. There's the friendship level, which can be a deep pain, depending on

the type of friendship, length of time, and trueness. The husband, or the wife's, death I find to be strange. First, a wife died that had been married to her husband for over a decade. Shortly after she left this world, the husband died due to their connection. This is the deepest and most meaningful death. Marriages between two people who truly love each other become one soul eventually. This is what is said to happen when people get married for all the right reasons. I find it to be true, because the two start thinking and sounding the same.

When two share in a sex session a little piece of soul goes with the other sex partner. (That's just a heads up for the one's not knowing.) Anyway, when a person is called home to the afterlife, people here on earth feel the separation. We look at death as being awful. Actually, we need to celebrate for the person running to their creator. We also need to pray for them that they will end up in the better of the two places. They'll have no more suffering to go through, no more tests to pass, or let downs. That's one form of death.

We hear about the gift of life everyday, too. Someone is having a new child as we speak. Life is precious and so uplifting, especially for a mother after all the pain she had to go through. At the end of the pain, she will say it was well worth it. The life of the baby brings so much joy to the eyes around them, along with relief to the parents after the baby has been determined healthy and well enough to go home. A party is given in order to shower the baby with gifts. A new member to the family has been welcomed in. The new life has brought the family together and has filled the room with love and smiles.

God gives us the gift of life. The devil comes in and tries to steal our gifts. The devil fills our heads up with lie after lie, telling us we're not loved, we're not worth

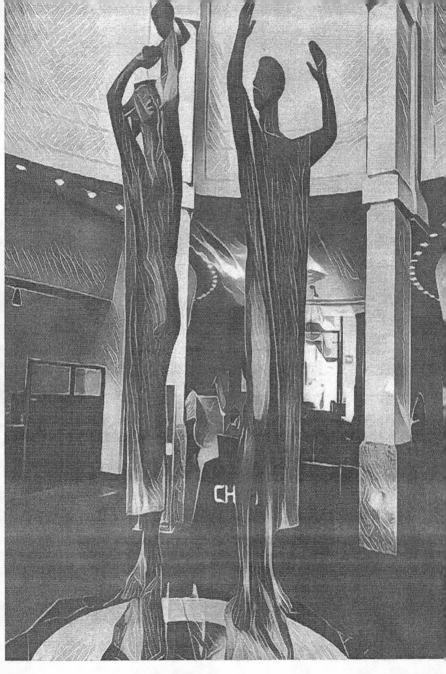

a pretty penny, kill yourself slowly, and join me here in hell. I know firsthand how the enemy comes in our heads and gets to work. He tells us we need the things of this world to be happy, when we don't. He leads us to believe he cares, and how by giving over our life would be the best choice, when all he does is cheat us of our lives God has planned for us. The enemy's job is to confuse us all day, every day.

He does a damn good job if you don't understand God's true way of living life. I thought I did, because I went to church every Sunday. I thought the devil couldn't touch me. I was wrong. I hadn't grasped how to use the weapons God provided me with. God's word explained to us how we must fight the devil with all the thinking power we have. Instead, I allowed myself to live like the confused folks. I started believing the lies being fed to me. I felt as if I was dying inside and I didn't think anyone knew. My mom didn't love me as much as I felt she should have. My father couldn't have loved me the way he smoked his drugs.

My spirit and emotions were becoming unbearable. I had my sister on my side when I needed a shoulder to lean on. She and I had our connections through a Higher Power. I could trust her in all aspects of my life. She and her two sons would accompany my son and me to church. We would meet up at church every Sunday, and we didn't miss a beat. I've been going to church ever since I could remember. I really never felt anything different about my life, as I compared it to the next person's. I had problems finding a decent job and home for my family. I saw myself living the same life my mother once lived, having different folks in and out of my son's life, and looking high and low for the one true love. Living in a shelter and all, I even slept in my car at one point, and I would drop my son with his grandparents. It was truly the pits.

I would continue to go to church no matter what the situation was. I continued believing in a God that is unseen, but felt He is real. I pictured God in my mind as not being able to see the wind, but I could feel it blow. I didn't understand why my life was so difficult. I kept on going in and out of jail, and my son didn't have much time to spend with his mother. On top of the heavy load of this world I was carrying, I was poor and lonely. There were people around me, but not the kind I needed to succeed. I wanted more out of life. I believed there was more to this life than what humans could offer me. My prayers began to change. When I would pray it was for understanding, knowledge, and peace of mind. I use to pray for money, a man, and a home, but when I did finally have those things I still wasn't at ease. This new prayer seemed to be what I needed and not what I wanted. Thank God for answering this new prayer.

I could remember it like it was yesterday, even though it was some odd years ago. I had just come home to my sister's house from jail. We were on our routine journey to church. The kids were sitting nicely enjoying the choir singing. I felt a feeling I never felt before, or maybe just hadn't noticed. The feeling was feeling of reassurance. The weight of the world seemed to have lifted off me. It was like I was the world, but I wasn't a part of the world. It was like God granted my prayers. There was this calmness about me that made me want more and more of God, and less and less bull crap.

From that day forward, I've been on a different type of mission. I wanted and needed to learn more about God, how he worked, how he thought, and how I could I have a relationship with him, a relationship with nothing but unconditional lasting love. I heard a lot about the things people said about God, but I needed something personal. I didn't get it right off the bat. I still had my old way of thinking. Things weren't coming to me as I planned, which made me turn to the world. I ended up in jail again, and this wasn't the same playful jail trip. I was super upset, because I thought I was on a new track.

The courts didn't give me a chance to change, but God did. The way I realized something good was going on in my life, showed in my actions. I stayed out of the mix and did me on a heavier scale. I was more focused on my son, and studying God's Word. When I was let out this time the spirit was on me tough. So much that the devil had no choice but to bow down. Actually, the way things were going around me were dreamlike. I knew what was going on before it would happen, and things were super clear. No one in my immediate circle was able to lie to me or annoy me. I felt super attentive to the issues around me. Something of a higher ability had been in my presence. I couldn't quite put my finger on what was happening, but I knew it was only by God's grace how the spirit allowed this knowledge to be shown to me. God didn't allow the tricks of this world to destroy his servant. My belief in God has protected and saved in many separate situations. I am, oh, so grateful!

I wanted the American Dream, a husband, two kids, and a house with a white picket fence. I thought the time had come for my dream life, simply because the man I was with treated me like a lady was supposed to be treated. I fell in love with all the back rubs, and nights spent out on the town. He had me feeling special as if I was already his wife, the only woman for him. We had a deep connection. I never wanted to let him go. We were going to be the happy-go-lucky family. I knew this was the man for me, until the spirit of this man allowed me to see the true him. It wasn't

what I wanted in my life. This man had down low secrets about his sex life, which I wanted no part of. I didn't find these things out about him for some time, as I continued to live life, I found out I wasn't the only one with problems that I had no idea on how to solve without God's help. We ended up breaking up. We would still see each other on different occasions, but I couldn't even look him in the eyes again. Our relationship took a road that had no light at the end. I was unable to get past this new information of his.

On one of our close to last encounters, we went to this bed and breakfast. I took a shower after our morning talk. I take long showers for the sake of a peaceful frame of mind. It seems as if it's my only escape from this world, plus I love to take my time starting my day. As I washed my body something happened. The Holy Spirit guided all my bodily actions. What I remembered was me just praising and thanking God but not on my own, there was a force behind the praise. I felt a sincere worship coming from within me. I couldn't stop washing up until I reached the top of my head to the tip of my toes, praising and more praising. I knew from that point this was what God wants from me on how to praise him. It made a lot of sense. It seemed as if the world only spoke on what not to do and what to do. The world's instructions pushed me to go through a rebellious stage. Having me think it was hard for me to please God. They were all wrong. God allowed me to learn the truth.

God doesn't need anything from us. He wants his due praise for being the one and only God, the only creator of every human being, sun, moon, and this earth. He deserves his praise when I wake up every morning, during my day, and again before bed. The feeling I received that morning at the bed and breakfast was one I wish I could always feel. It was awesome! I pray you get a chance to feel it.

I didn't turn into a perfect human after my encounter. As a matter of fact, I went back to jail. This time it was for being homeless. I collected $325 for my son from the government, but babysat for my sister in a different county. I had my son enrolled in the same school as her children. Well, the government found out, and called this a case of fraud. I removed my son from that school, and talked to my sister about the problem. My sister assured me it was cool, but I had to find out the hard way. I ended up with a warrant for my arrest, but I didn't think it was serious. So, I moved leaving the warrant over my head. I forgot about my spiritual encounter. I continued to live in the flesh.

I never stopped asking and praying for God's help. Things were okay, but I knew they could have been better. I had settled

for less month after month. I was sick of the new area I lived in. I left my so-called friends behind but I allowed them to drag me back to my uncomfortable lifestyle. I went back to the old neighborhood unprepared, and ended up in jail on the account of the warrant. I was in shock from the awful jail treatment, but I guess I forgot how the jail cages people up like animals all day. I stayed in prayer and attended any, and every, Godly service. I knew this life wasn't for a person with my strong belief in God. I needed to learn how God would want me to live. I knew my thoughts were not lining up with the righteous folk. I wanted and needed a change in my life, and in my thinking. I couldn't take or do another temporary jail stay. This jail crap was death staring me straight in the soul of my eyes. I needed to find my way out and stay out. It didn't happen as I had planned.

I was released from jail with nothing.

The money I had, I spent it during my jail stay. I had two cars and sold one to make ends meet. I looked for a job and went to church. Still I couldn't get things in order. God knew I was tired of living according to what the world had to offer. God wasn't finished working with me. I thank him for all that he's done, and is doing for me. God works in many different ways. I met this guy who needed a roommate and I needed a place to stay. I made money to pay my part of the rent and bills. That wasn't the problem; the problem was the illegal way of paying. I knew this and God knew it too. I felt like my life was okay for the time being, and improving day by day. I'm glad God had other plans for my life. This was to know him on a personal level. That thought led me to letting go of everything unrighteous I learned which didn't pertain to God... basically, 30 years of worldly living in my 32-year old life.

I had to start fresh. I needed a new way of thinking. Thoughts of guidance had become my mission. I knew I needed to become a mature woman. I was a role model on how to be the best gang member and jawbreaker. Now, it was a different time in my life. I felt the need to become a positive role model. The only way that would come about is if I gave my entire life over to the true Master, owner of the world, our heavenly God. The devil may be making mischief for us in this world by feeding us lies and showing us the temporary glitz and glamour, the things that can't satisfy the soul. This is the reason I searched higher, for a sense of peace. I'm glad God works on his time and not on ours. I could have been driven crazy believing the lies this world has to offer. There are signs placed all around us from above this world, showing us there is a higher existence. If and when we believe, we'll be able to understand them.

For example, we have to have food to live on earth. We also need food to live in the Spirit, which is God's unchanging word. To live a balanced life it is necessary to have order in our life. I was completely lost without the correct direction to move toward until I found religion. Religion has many different labels. It's hard to say which one is the correct one. The forefathers of Abraham continued by Moses, who brought the Ten Commandments, which came straight from the heavens, founded Judaism. The Jewish community believes in nothing but the Torah (Old Testament) of the Holy Bible. Their worshipping days start on Friday night, until Saturday. Then the Christian Religion, which was founded by Christ, who brought with Him the Holy Spirit, and the New Testament of The Holy Bible. Christians also believe in the Old Testament of the Holy Bible. They worship on Sundays. Muhammad founded the faith of Islam. In turn, Abraham believed in monotheism, meaning belief in only one God. Abraham was the first actual Muslim. The word "Muslim" means being submissive to God. Muslim's believe in the Holy Quran. One man, Muhammad, wrote the Quran. This was sent down through the Angel Gabriel. Muslims worship on Fridays. There are a few more religions that serve only God.

What's a trip is all these religions are separated because of the titles and the way they worship. The basis of all these religions is basically the same: believing and loving one God. I've studied a little of each, and I received something from each of these faiths. They all motivated me to worship God. They also had me to come to this conclusion of just being a believer. Worshipping one God is enough to allow a person to be inspired to change, for his or her betterment.

There are faith organizations that discuss and meet all the time. This meeting is called an interfaith session. Interfaith is actually how we gather information from each other on how to worship our one true God, the unseen awesome God. It's a beautiful thing. I pray this reading has inspired you to search within yourself revealing the true you. Find God then you'll be able to live life with the full human excellence God has instilled in you. A person should enjoy the life they live here on earth. Now go out and live your life with the utmost respect for God, the one God who only wants good in your life. May your lifelong journey be safe and lovable. You can do this. Believe in yourself at all times. You can have the benefits of this life by being true to yourself, having patience and remaining firm. May God be with you and yours. Let your inner man live and let go of that outer material made by man. Put that person to rest!